Kimbrel Goes To School

by Auntie Kim

PublishAmerica
Baltimore

First printing

ISBN: 978-1-4560-4892-1
PUBLISHED BY PUBLISHAMERICA, LLLP
www.publishamerica.com
Baltimore

Printed in the United States of America

Dedication

I dedicate this book to my nephew, Isaiah N. Summers for your assistance and wisdom.

To Mikiah M. Summers, my niece, my sister, Vette, and Aunt Ellen, thank you for your love and devotion as well as keeping me anchored.

Lastly, to my dad, Cleveland, I appreciate you for doing the grunt work without ever complaining and teaching me how to streamline my thoughts. Nancy, my mom, cheerleader, advisor and friend, I dedicate this book to you for constantly encouraging me to believe in the Creator who stretches my abilities beyond it's familiarity to attain the impossibility.

Acknowledgements

I honor God for allowing my gifts to make room for me. A Loving regard to my loved ones and friends whom have supported me throughout life's journey. I would like to acknowledge a few people for making it possible for me to connect with my audience.

I am grateful to Publish America for giving me this opportunity, Lisa J. Hicks for suggesting I start my writing career appealing to young readers, my editors, Marla D. McAllister, Mrs. Laura McLean and Professor Michelle R. Horton. Thank you, Shafi Mustafa, Managing Director, of SMMC Studios, LLC for creating the Auntie Kim brand. A special thanks to Jihad A. Edwards, for your kindness, collaboration and strength. I am deeply gratified to Professor Michelle R. Horton, for your seamless efforts in facilitating the presentation of the Auntie Kim brand as well as the clean up you did behind the scenes.

Greetings from Auntie Kim

I would like to say a special hello to the readers of this book. I think you are extraordinary and I am excited about the individual that you are going to grow up to become. Thank you for allowing me to come into your home and school to visit with you for a little while. I hope you enjoy this series.

Love,

Auntie Kim

Summer break was ending and the children were excited to go back to school. Kimbrel was especially excited, because she had a birthday that summer. This meant she was finally able to start school just like her older sister and cousins.

It was the day before the first day of school and Kimbrel had so much to do! She had to go to the mall to pick up some items, to prepare for the most important day of her life. Kimbrel asked her older sister, Kwan, to help her write a checklist. She did not want to forget anything.

Check List
Dress
Shoes
Bookbag

Kimbrel's checklist was all complete and she was ready to go shopping. Dad, Mom, Kwan and Kimbrel got in the car and headed to the mall.

When they arrived at the Mall, they split up. Dad took Kwan to find the items on her list and Mom took Kimbrel to find the items on Kimbrel's list.

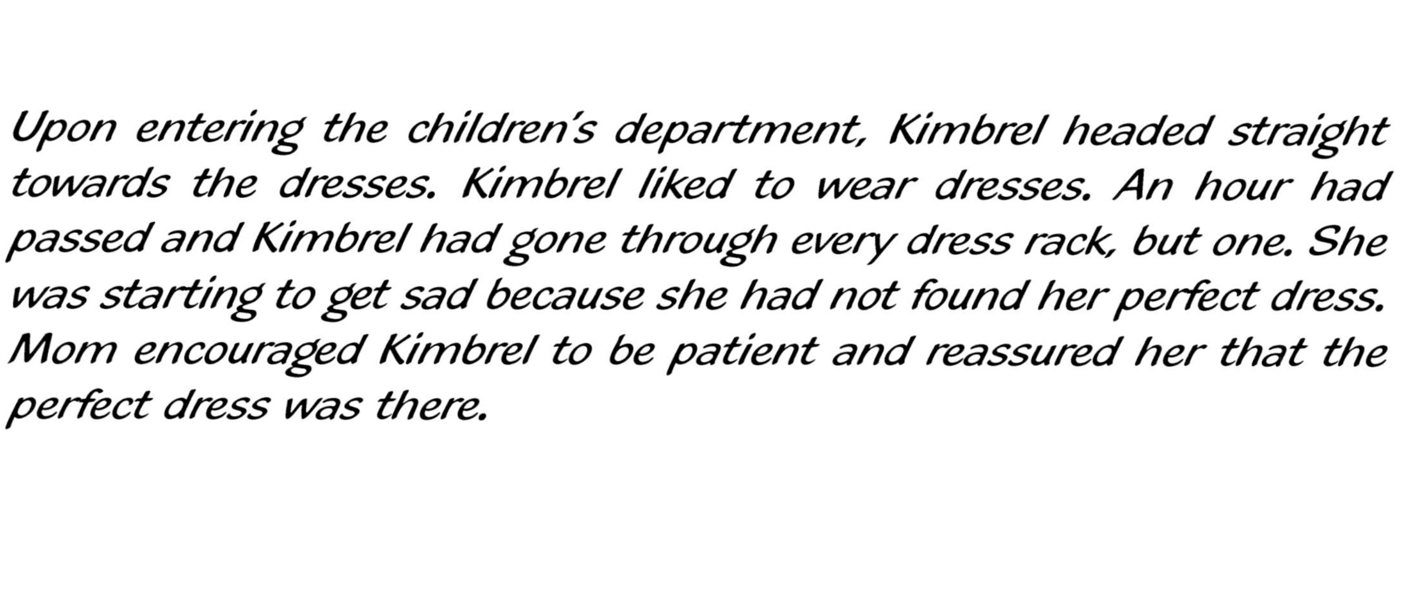

Upon entering the children's department, Kimbrel headed straight towards the dresses. Kimbrel liked to wear dresses. An hour had passed and Kimbrel had gone through every dress rack, but one. She was starting to get sad because she had not found her perfect dress. Mom encouraged Kimbrel to be patient and reassured her that the perfect dress was there.

Kimbrel walked over to the last dress rack and went through each dress very slowly. Suddenly, a light purple dress with a hot pink collar caught her eye. Kimbrel knew instantly that the light purple dress was her perfect dress. She shouted to her mom, "I found it! This is the dress!"

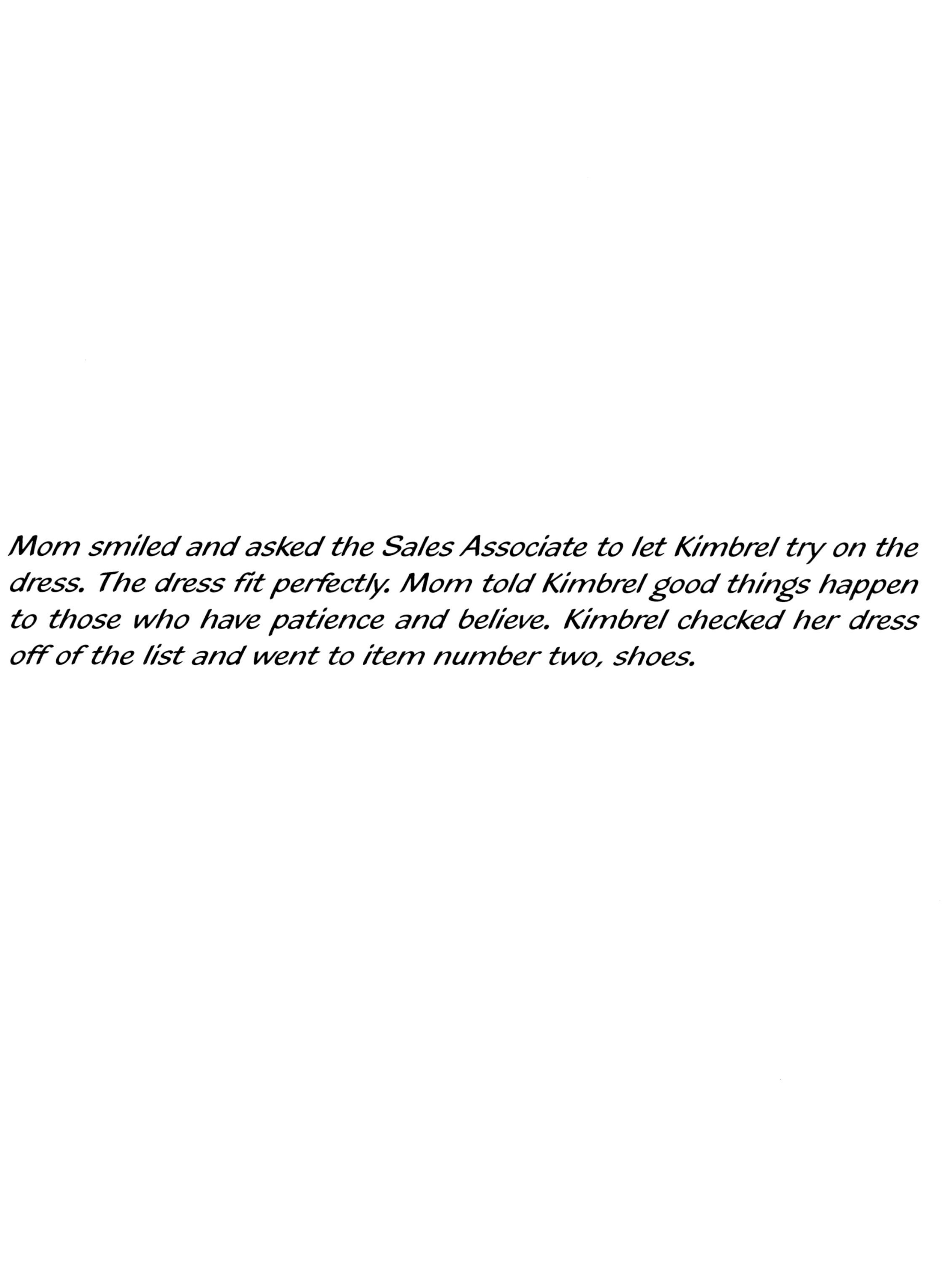

Mom smiled and asked the Sales Associate to let Kimbrel try on the dress. The dress fit perfectly. Mom told Kimbrel good things happen to those who have patience and believe. Kimbrel checked her dress off of the list and went to item number two, shoes.

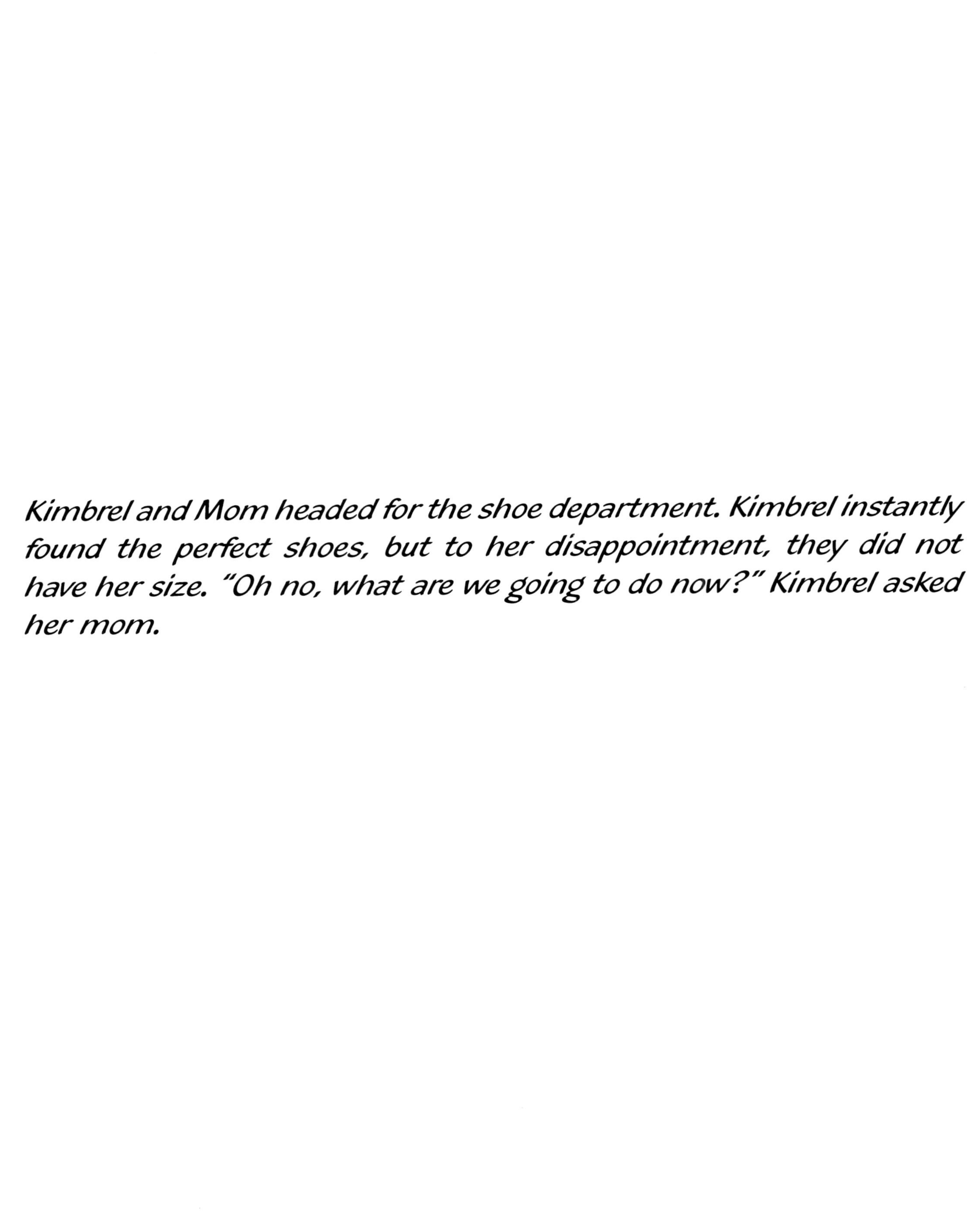

Kimbrel and Mom headed for the shoe department. Kimbrel instantly found the perfect shoes, but to her disappointment, they did not have her size. "Oh no, what are we going to do now?" Kimbrel asked her mom.

Mom kneeled down in front of Kimbrel and spoke very gently. "Kimbrel, do you believe that we are going to find shoes that will match your perfect dress?"

"Yes, mommy I believe!" Kimbrel said to her mom. Mom asked Kimbrel. "What is the most important thing you need to do?" Kimbrel thought and thought and thought.

All of a sudden it came to her. "I know I need to have patience!" Mom was proud of Kimbrel for remembering what to do when she is expecting something big.

Mom and Kimbrel left the store and sat down on a bench. They put on their thinking caps to locate Kimbrel's perfect shoes.

What do you think mom and Kimbrel came up with? Put a check next to your answer below and color the pictures when you finish reading the story.

☐ *They went home.*

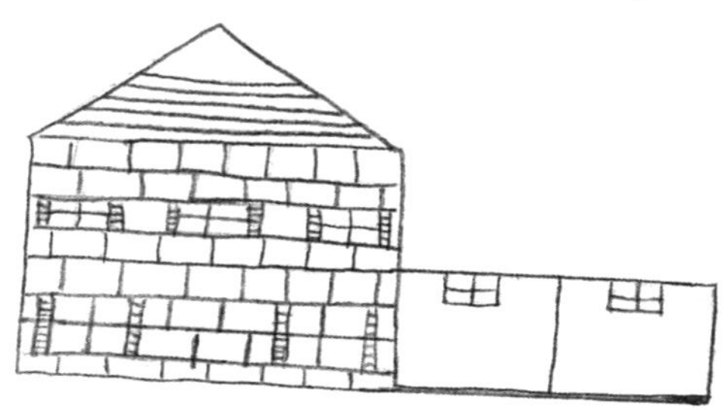

☐ *Kimbrel and Mom went to another store.*

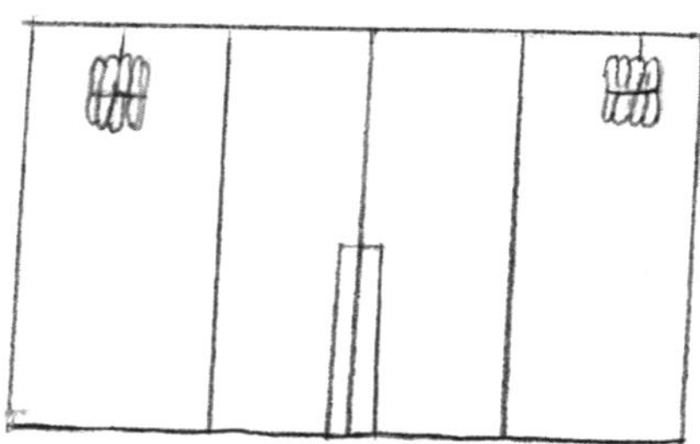

☐ *Kimbrel began to cry and mom comforted her.*

That's right! Kimbrel and Mom went to another store. When they arrived, Kimbrel believed that she would find shoes to match her perfect dress. Mom and Kimbrel took their time going through all of the selections. As Mom looked up, she found the same shoes that were in the other store. She gave them to Kimbrel and they fit! Mom purchased the shoes. She and Kimbrel set out for their last adventure to find the final item on Kimbrel's list.

Can you guess the last item on Kimbrel's list? Put a check mark next to your picture below and color the pictures once you are finish reading the story.

☐ *Dress*

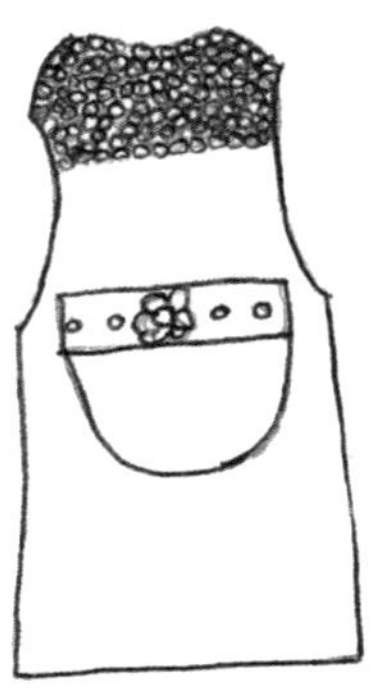

☐ *Book Bag*

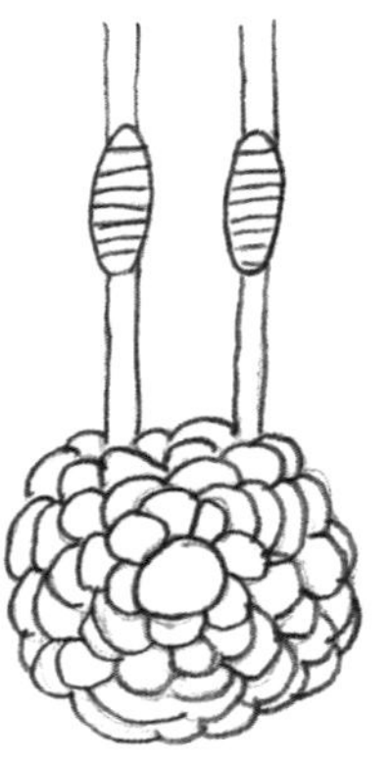

☐ *Shoes*

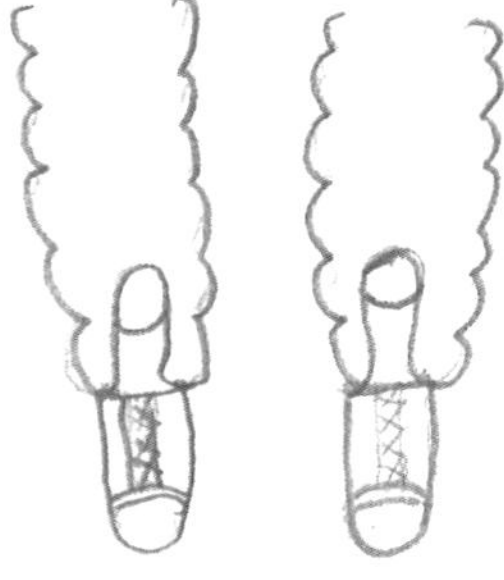

Good job! Kimbrel and Mom were looking for a book bag for Kimbrel. They went to the back- to- school section to find the perfect book bag. Kimbrel went through the entire pile to find her book bag. After Kimbrel pulled it out of the big pile, she tried it on in front of the mirror. Mom paid for it and they were off to find Dad and Kwan to go home.

When they arrived home, Kwan showed Mom and Kimbrel all of her purchases. Kimbrel took her bags and went in her room. She came out wearing her new dress, shoes and book bag. Kimbrel liked to get new clothes and shoes. Every time Kimbrel went shopping, she would always model her new clothes and shoes for Kwan, Dad and Mom.

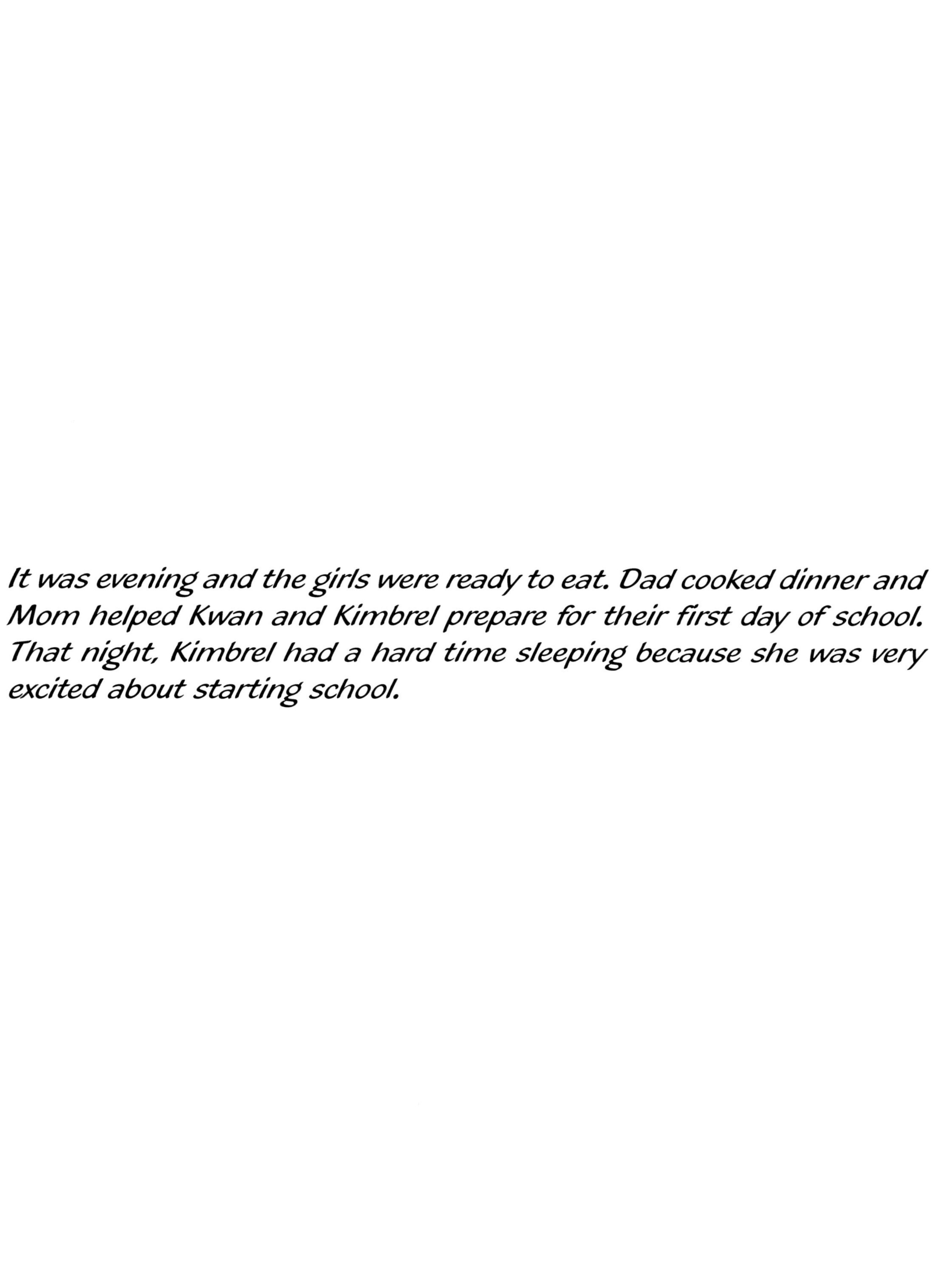

It was evening and the girls were ready to eat. Dad cooked dinner and Mom helped Kwan and Kimbrel prepare for their first day of school. That night, Kimbrel had a hard time sleeping because she was very excited about starting school.

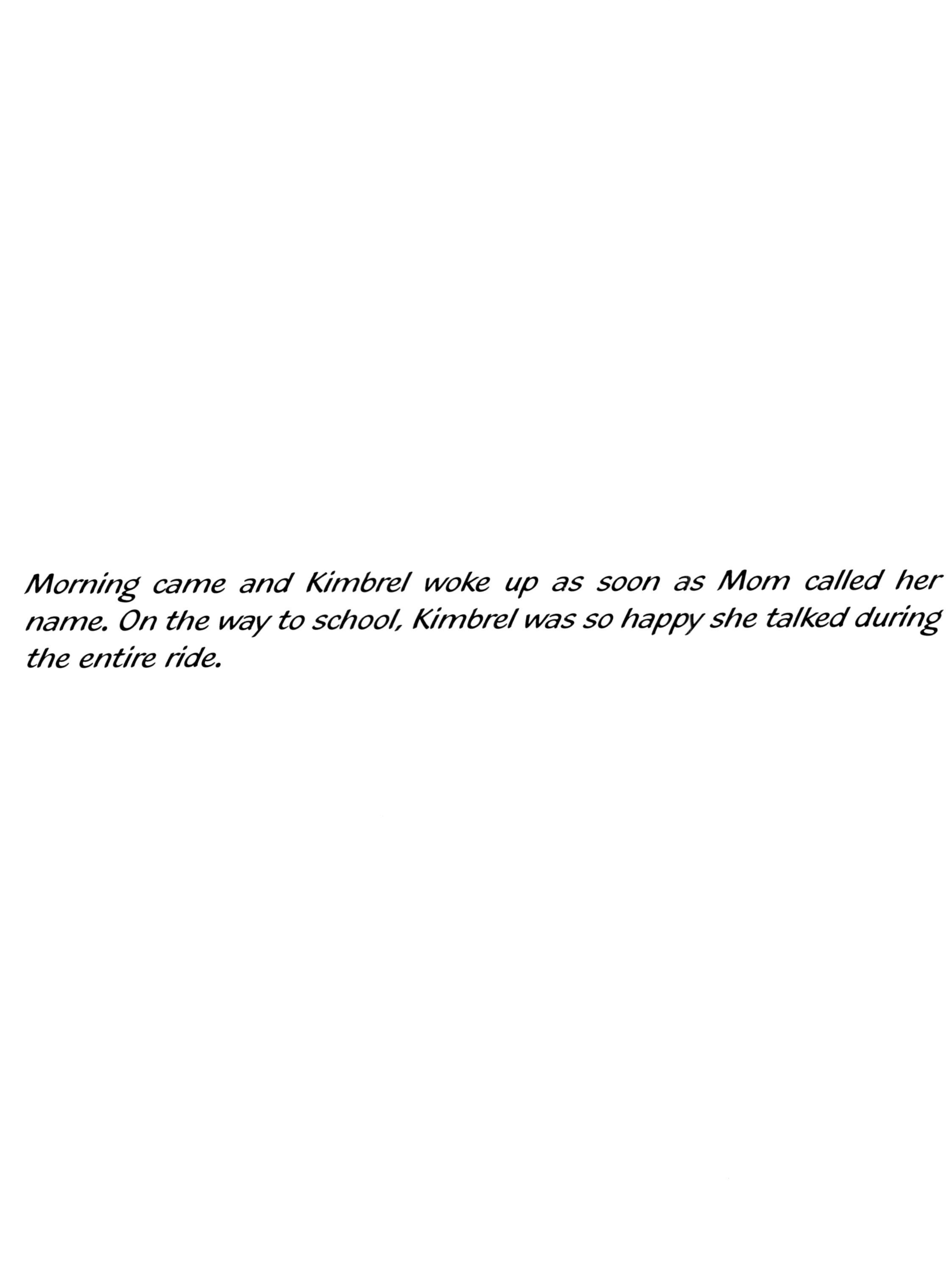

Morning came and Kimbrel woke up as soon as Mom called her name. On the way to school, Kimbrel was so happy she talked during the entire ride.

When they arrived, Kimbrel got her book bag and walked in with Kwan and Mom. Kimbrel was a little nervous, but did not focus on that because she had been waiting for that moment for an entire year. Mom and Kwan walked Kimbrel to her class. Kimbrel hugged Mom and Kwan and walked in her classroom.

She was greeted by a tall lady. The lady had kind eyes and introduced herself as Ms. Brown, the teacher's assistant. Ms. Brown showed Kimbrel where to hang her book bag and told her to find a seat at any of the tables.

Kimbrel sat down next to a girl named Lucinda. Kimbrel was very friendly and they immediately began talking. They were having so much fun until other children came over to join them. The table got filled instantly.

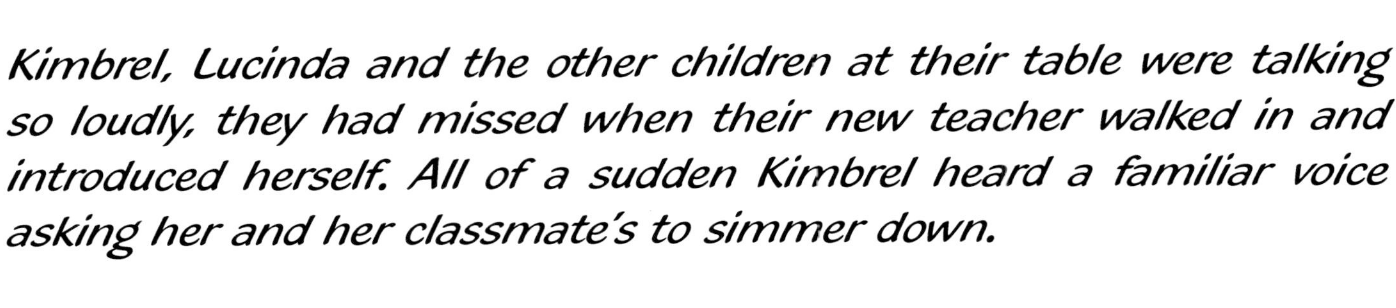

Kimbrel, Lucinda and the other children at their table were talking so loudly, they had missed when their new teacher walked in and introduced herself. All of a sudden Kimbrel heard a familiar voice asking her and her classmate's to simmer down.

Kimbrel quickly closed her mouth, sat back in her seat and thought to herself, oh no! It couldn't be! She slowly turned her head to see whose familiar voice was standing at the chalkboard.

Kimbrel recognized the shoes her new teacher was wearing, her legs and dress. Can you guess who Kimbrel's new teacher was? Please check your answer below and color the picture when you finish reading the story.

☐ *Kimbrel's nurse*

☐ *Kimbrel's dentist*

☐ *Kimbrel's mom*

That's right! Kimbrel's new teacher was Mrs. Johnson, Kimbrel's mom.

Questions:

Do you think Kimbrel was happy that her mom was her new Pre-K Teacher?
How would you feel if your mom was your Pre-K Teacher?
Would you want to share her with your other classmates?
How do you think Kimbrel handled her mom being her Pre –K Teacher?

If you want to send Kimbrel or Auntie Kim a message, you can do so at www.auntiekim.net

If you enjoyed reading about Kimbrel Goes To School; please look out for Auntie Kim's Kimbrel Learns To Share.

Good bye for now until the next time.